ACKNOWLEDGEMENTS

I wish to express my deepest appreciation to those that made contributions to this work by continuously offering encouragement, insight, and guidance.

I would like to dedicate this book to my family, friends, and those who have walked along side of me throughout my Leadership Experiences. I will forever be grateful to God for the courage and people He has given me as support on this journey.

Also, to my student leaders, remember every choice you are allowed to make is an opportunity for you to exercise your leadership skills. Do not be afraid but choose wisely balancing your character with your intellect.

Lastly, to my co-founder, what started as a vision has slowly become reality. Our talents and passion for positively impacting students' lives through 21st century skills are changing the world.

> "I alone cannot change the world, but I can cast a stone across the waters to create many ripples."
> -Mother Teresa

CONTENT

Introduction	Welcome to the Student Leadership Experience Your Leadership Journey Project	
Essential #1	Work Smart	6
Essential #2	Respond Smart	25
Essential #3	Smart Goals	28
Essential #4	Plan Smart	33
Essential #5	Smart Victories	37
Essential #6	Smart Talk	42
Essential #7	Smart Life	46
Essential #8	Brave Voice	48
Bonus Lesson	A Different MindS.E.T.: Student Entrepreneurs of Tomorrow	51
Developing a Winner's Attitude	Impulse Control Social/Emotional Intelligence Gratitude Grit	64 70 73 75
Glossary		77
References		80
Assessments	Leadership Experience Assessment Leadership Experience Parent Survey Leadership Experience Teacher Survey	82 83 84

WHY STUDENT LEADERSHIP EXPERIENCE?

Our 21st century educational system continues to be dominated with 19th century skills such as memorizing facts and producing isolated projects. However, can you imagine a classroom of students eager to collaborate with their peers about ways to resolve every day challenges and students learning effective communication skills, such as active listening and speaking, emotional intelligence, goal-setting, and the power of critical thinking and creativity? These skills are the foundation of **The Student Leadership Experience,** which results in academic achievement as well as necessities for college and career success. So how might we create this holistic learning experience for our students?

Here's how it works!
Students learn leadership skills from this book during weekly lessons conducted to support a growth mindset of:
- Collaboration
- Strategic Thinking
- Goal-Setting/College and Career success
- Problem-Solving/Grit
- Public Speaking
- Entrepreneurial Skills
- Critical Thinking with Legos
- Social and Emotional Intelligence
- And much more

Results!
Success is measured by rubrics and multiple assessments used throughout the book. The goals of the Student Leadership Experience are to increase the number of 3rd grade students reading on grade level, increase the number of students prepared with training skills for the work force, as well as improve the number of students attending and graduating from college.

Working towards these goals will help produce an actively engaged community of students who are determined to reach their highest potential with an awareness that success is limitless all while respecting others.

These outcomes are my passion for education. Writing this book is my effort to expand this opportunity for many students. For this reason, I urge you to participate in the Student Leadership Experience. Not only will it positively affect your students but also with a domino effect, it will positively impact your community.

YOUR LEADERSHIP JOURNEY PROJECT

Life is a marathon, not a sprint...Train for endurance not speed. —Unknown

All student leaders will be responsible for writing three pieces on their own "Leadership Story", a piece at the beginning, middle, and end of the program. These pieces should reflect their research, knowledge and growth as a leader throughout the program including examples of leaders and new insight on strategies for success. The final or 3rd leadership piece will be a written essay prepared to share with peers during the last few weeks of the program. Expectations for the third writing piece can be found within the last essential, Essential #8- Brave Voice. The Brave Voice Rubric should be distributed at least 3 months in advance.

1st Leadership story: This story should be written at the **beginning** of the program including at least two paragraphs.
In your own words: What is a leader? Explain any challenges or successes you have had as a leader? What would you like to learn about leadership?

2nd Leadership story: This story should be written during the **middle** of the program including at least four paragraphs.
In your own words: What is a leader? Explain any challenges or successes you have had as a leader? What new strategies have you learned about leadership? Research and share an example of a person who is an effective leader and explain why you chose this person.

3rd Leadership story: This story should be written **before the end** of the program including at least six paragraphs. *See essential #8-Brave Voice*
In your own words: How have you grown as a leader? What challenges have you had and resolved as a leader? Explain your greatest strength as a leader. What have you learned from this program that can help you gain success throughout your future?

LEADERSHIP ESSENTIALS

ESSENTIAL #1

WORK SMART

I value working with others. When I work on a team to complete a task, I seek out others of different cultures, strengths, and personalities. I know together we can be smarter and better than we are alone. I don't let differences hinder a smart solution.

Helpful quotes about working smart:

Alone we are smart. Together we are brilliant.
—Steven Anderson

Love is appreciating your differences as well as your similarities. —Unknown

It's amazing how much you can accomplish when it doesn't matter who get the credit. —Unknown

Individually we are one drop. But together, we are an ocean.
—Ryunosuke Sator

ESSENTIAL QUESTION: WHAT ARE THE SECRETS OF A GREAT TEAM?

Objective: To develop social and emotional skills that will allow students to work effectively while thinking critically and creatively with diverse groups.

Purpose: Students will be challenged with the task of practicing effective communication, collaboration, and cooperation skills.

Vocabulary: Teamwork

Materials: Self-Assessment/Team Building Rubric.
Essential Skill #1-overview and quotes
Our Community
Whole Leader
Team building day schedule (example)
Animal Personality test

Directions:
1. Read overview and quotes for Essential Skill #1
2. Allow students to discuss with a partner about their favorite quote and explain why. Allow four students to share whole group until all quotes have been discussed.
3. Review vocabulary terms as they relate to overview
4. Review the team building schedule and Self-Assessment
4. See Team Building Attachment

Tip: Encourage students to devise a plan and work as a group to complete the task. Do not reveal answers until time is up.

Conclusion/Evaluation: Complete Self-Assessment / Team Building Rubric. Reflect as a whole group the challenges, successes, and lessons learned about the importance of working as a team. All reflections should be recorded in their student reflection notebook.

TEAM BUILDING ACTIVITIES DESCRIPTION

Our Community (sharing, understanding, personality values)
Individuals will sign their names in the boxes that represent them. Each person may sign only one box. This will help individuals identify similarities and differences in the group to determine ways to strengthen how the group works together.

Human Shuffle (Team dynamics, setting and achieving a goal, problem-solving)
Students will be divided into two teams. Each team will stand on a board facing one another. All students will need to work together to achieve the goal. Students will move forward on the board to ultimately change places exactly to create a mirror effect. For example, the third student in line on the right side should eventually be the third student on the left side of the path. The task is over once the group has made a mirror reflection.

Animal Personality (leadership strengths and areas of growth and diversity)
Students will listen and follow directions to complete a student appropriate personality test. Students will also work in groups to discuss personality strengths and weaknesses.

3D Lego Activity (identify strengths in others and work critically/ collaboratively as a group)
Students work in groups to construct a 3D Lego model. Only one person at a time can view the model. Once the group starts to design the Lego model exactly as the model in the next room, no one from the group can view it again. If the model is correct, then the task is complete.

Trust Walk (physical and fun)
Students will pair up with a partner. On signal, students will take a walk, blindfolded, throughout the building being led by their trusted partner. Once the pair reaches the half-way point they will switch roles, (exchange blindfold) and continue to the ending destination.

Cooperation Squares (problem solving, communication, perseverance)
Student will be given puzzle pieces to create five squares. Students must work together to create five squares without talking using their puzzle pieces.

Cup Stack Challenge (problem solving and collaboration)
Students will work in groups using 10 Solo cups to build a pyramid without touching the cups. Only one rubber band with five 4-inch string attached are allowed for maneuvering the cups.

Spaghetti Tower Challenge
Students will work in groups of 2-4 to build the tallest tower possible using 20 spaghetti noodles, one foot of tape, one foot of string, and a marshmallow. Students can use the materials in any way but the marshmallow must be on top of the tower.

Copyright @ 2016 [Patricia L. Russell, ED.S]. All Rights Reserved.
This material is not to be used or duplicated without consent from Patricia L. Russell.

STUDENT LEADERS OUR COMMUNITY

Invite individuals to sign their name inside a box that fits their description. Each person may only sign one box.

I am an only child	I play on a sports team	I have never been camping	I have traveled to another country	I have lots of sisters and brothers	I have blue eyes
I wear glasses	I have a pet	I am very shy	I play a musical instrument	I speak more than one language fluently	I am a girl
I moved here from a different country or state	I have a family member in the armed forces	I enjoy reading	I am or have been a Girl Scout or Boy Scout	I was born in this community	I make friends easily
I am left-handed	I know how to cook	I am the oldest child in my family	I sing in a choir	I am the youngest child in my family	I wear socks to bed
I have won an award	I have chores on the weekend	I love scary movies	My favorite color is orange	I can draw very well	I have a messy bedroom

Name _____

Date _____

ESSENTIALS #1

FACILITATOR

WELCOME TO STUDENT LEADERSHIP TEAM BUILDING DAY!

Established Goals/State Standards(s): Academic Development:
CCSS. ELA – Literacy SL.3.1 Engage effectively in a range of collaborative discussions (One-On-One, in groups, and teacher-led) with diverse partners on grade level topics and texts, building on others' ideas and expressing their own clearly. (CCSS.ELA-Literacy. SL.3.1b)

Career Development: Standard 4.6-Students will demonstrate ability to work in teams.

Personal/Social Development: Standard 7.5 – use effective listening skills

Goals: Work together as a team
Listened to others' ideas
Clearly expressed your ideas

Station 1: "Human Shuffle"
Did you work together with others as a team? 👍👎
Did you listen to others' ideas? 👍👎
Did you clearly express your ideas? 👍👎

Station 2: "The Whole Leader"
Did you work together with others as a team? 👍👎
Did you listen to others' ideas? 👍👎
Did you clearly express your ideas? 👍👎

Station 3: "Spaghetti Tower"
Did you work together with others as a team? 👍👎
Did you listen to others' ideas? 👍👎
Did you clearly express your ideas? 👍👎

Station 4: "Cup Stack Challenge"
Did you work together with others as a team? 👍👎
Did you listen to others' ideas? 👍👎
Did you clearly express your ideas? 👍👎

- **What did you learn about yourself and leadership today?**

Copyright @ 2016 [Patricia L. Russell, ED.S]. All Rights Reserved.
This material is not to be used or duplicated without consent from Patricia L. Russell.

WELCOME TO STUDENT LEADERSHIP TEAMBUILDING DAY!

All students will complete a timed activity at each station. When you hear the timer, please stop and prepare to reflect on learned information.

Career Development: Standard 4.6-Students will demonstrate ability to work in teams.

Personal/Social Development: Standard 7.5 – use effective listening skills

Goals: Work together as a team
Listened to others' ideas
Clearly expressed your ideas

Station 1: "Human Shuffle"
Did you work together with others as a team?
Did you listen to others ideas?
Did you clearly express your ideas?

Station 2: "The Whole Leader"
Did you work together with others as a team?
Did you listen to others ideas?
Did you clearly express your ideas?

Station 3: "Spaghetti Tower"
Did you work together with others as a team?
Did you listen to others ideas?
Did you clearly express your ideas?

Station 4: "Cup Stack Challenge"
Did you work together with others as a team?
Did you listen to others ideas?
Did you clearly express your ideas?

- What did you learn about yourself and leadership today?

THE WHOLE LEADER

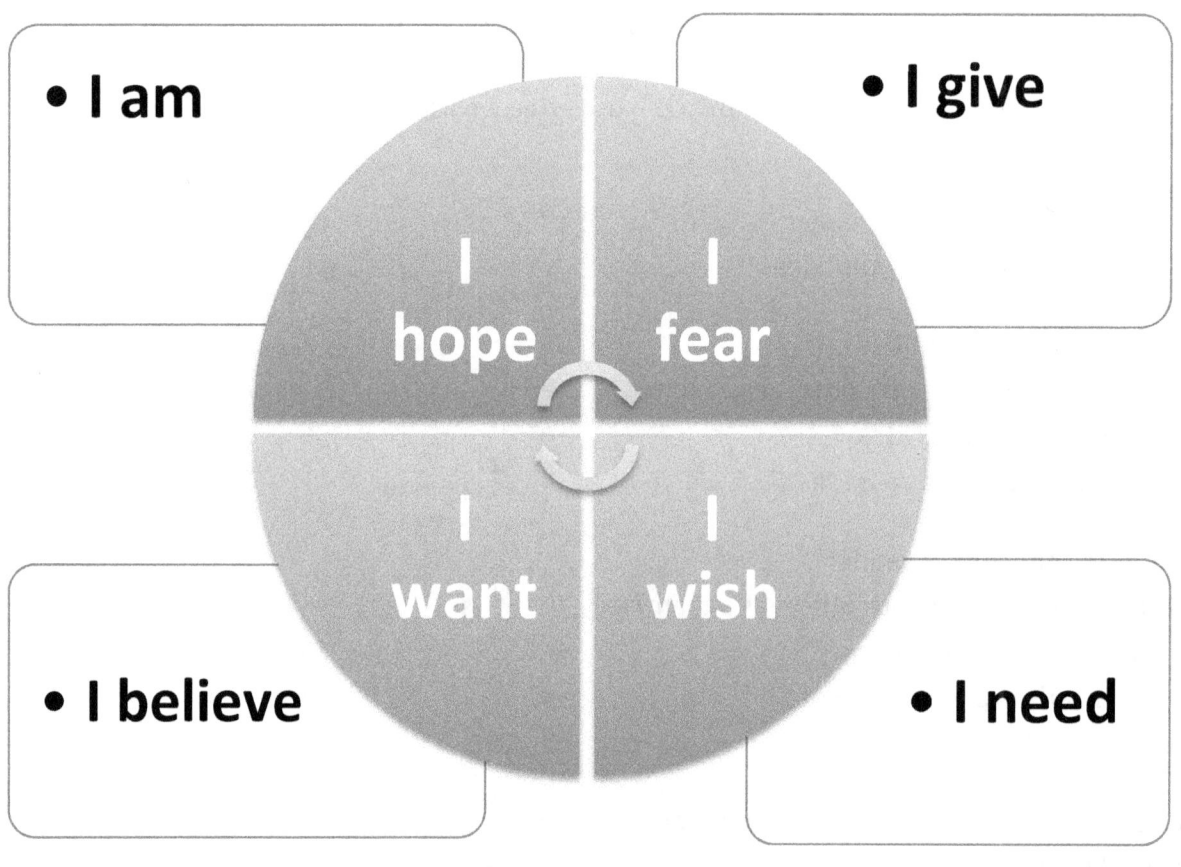

COOPERATION SQUARES

Make a copy of each template and cut the square into parts. Mark envelopes A-E and distribute the pieces: Envelope A: All A pieces; Envelope B: all B pieces, etc...

Make as many copies of the template as you plan to have small groups. If you have five groups, you will need five sets of templates. You will also need that many sets of envelopes. The pieces will last longer if they are copied on card stock.

Give each small group a set of envelopes A-E. They are to communicate non-verbally and create five complete squares. (These will match your original template.) Directions may also include the fact that each square will only be made of three parts, a letter may be used only one time in a square, and not all letters will be used each time. How much you explain will depend of the grade level of the group you are teaching.

After completing the task, have a discussion about what worked well, what didn't work and other components of cooperation. This can also be used as an activity on communication and can be done in conjunction with a similar activity done verbally, with discussion being whether or not the non-verbal or verbal worked better and why.

COOPERATION SQUARES

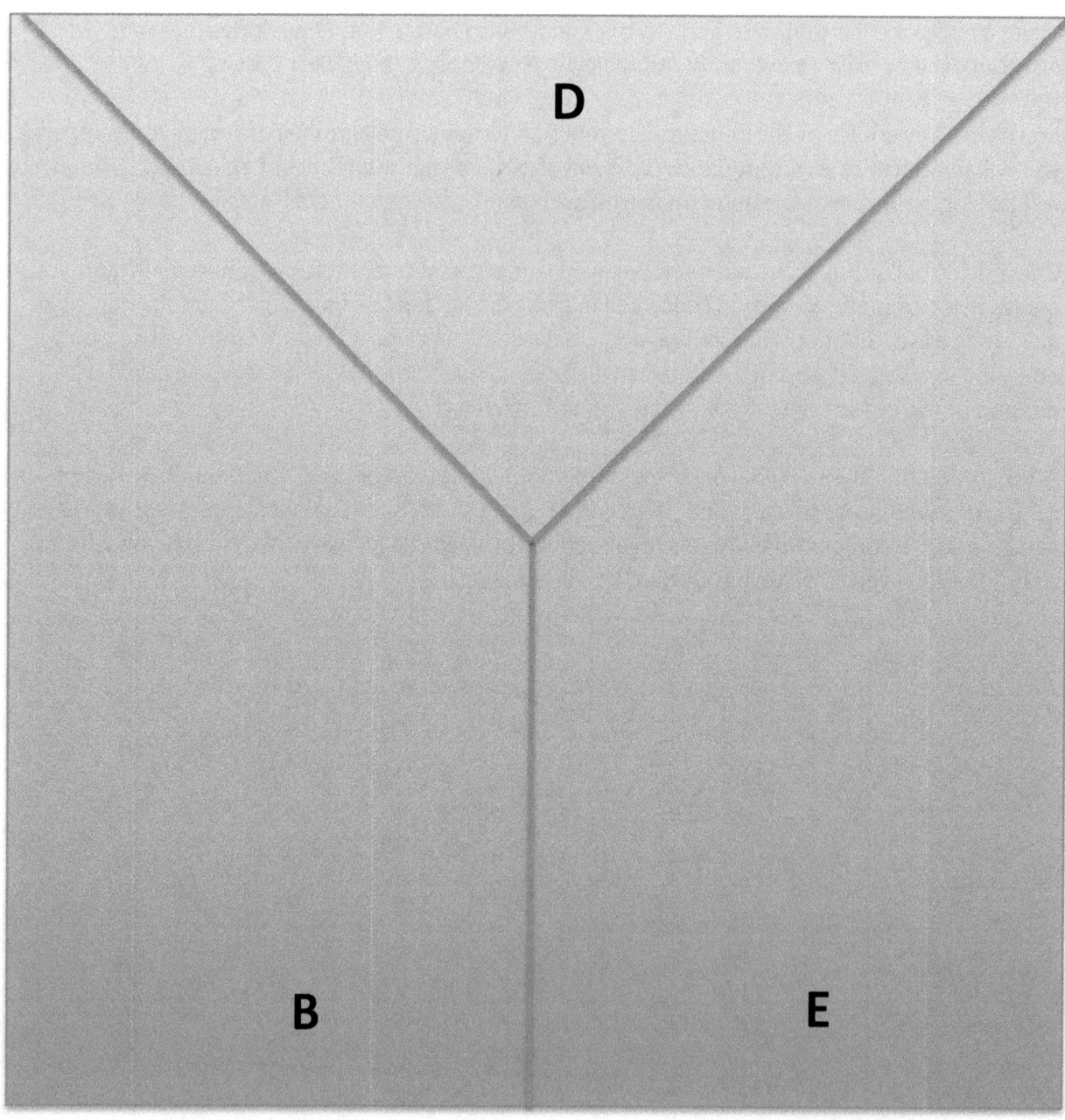

COOPERATION SQUARES

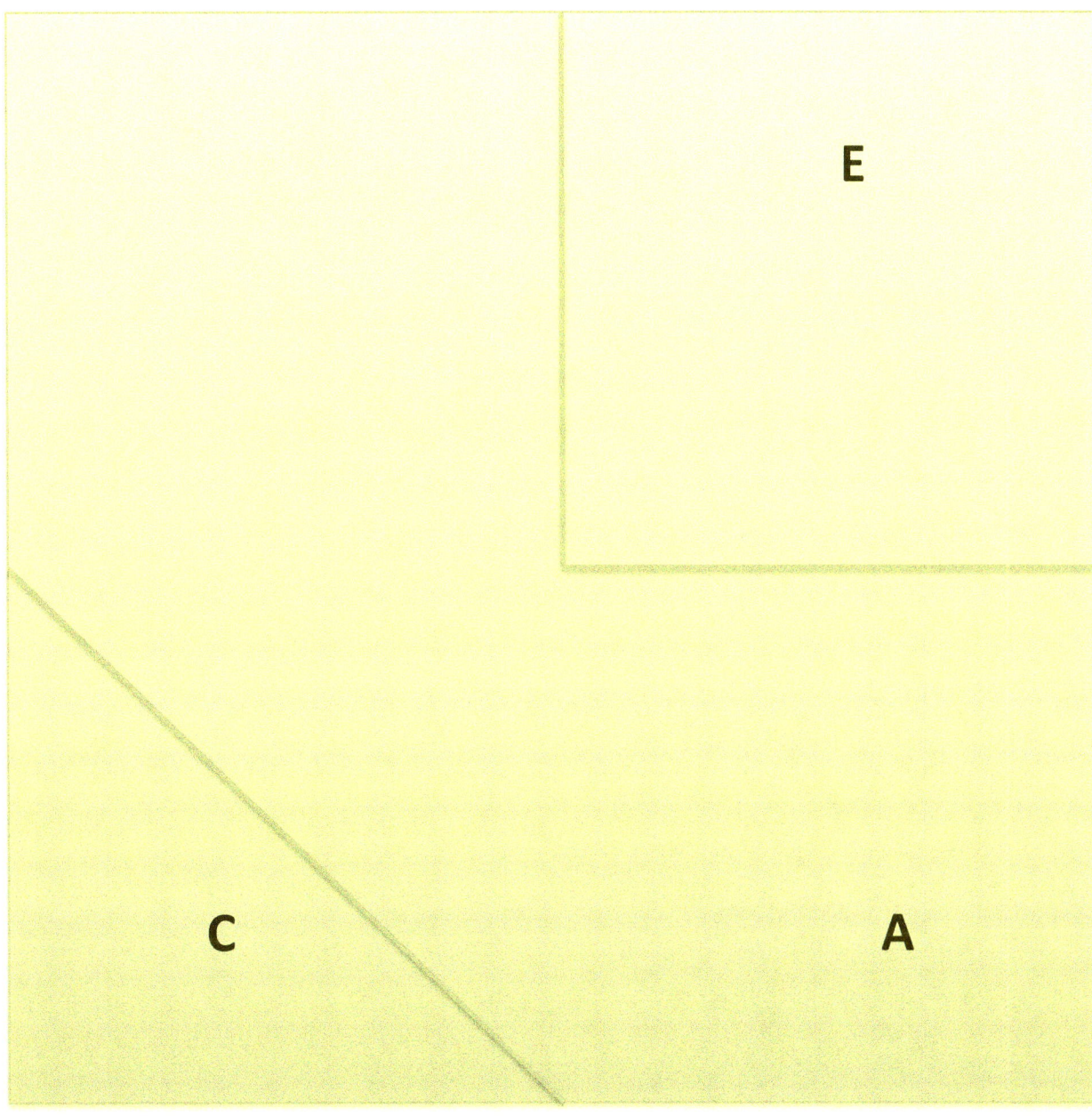

COOPERATION SQUARES

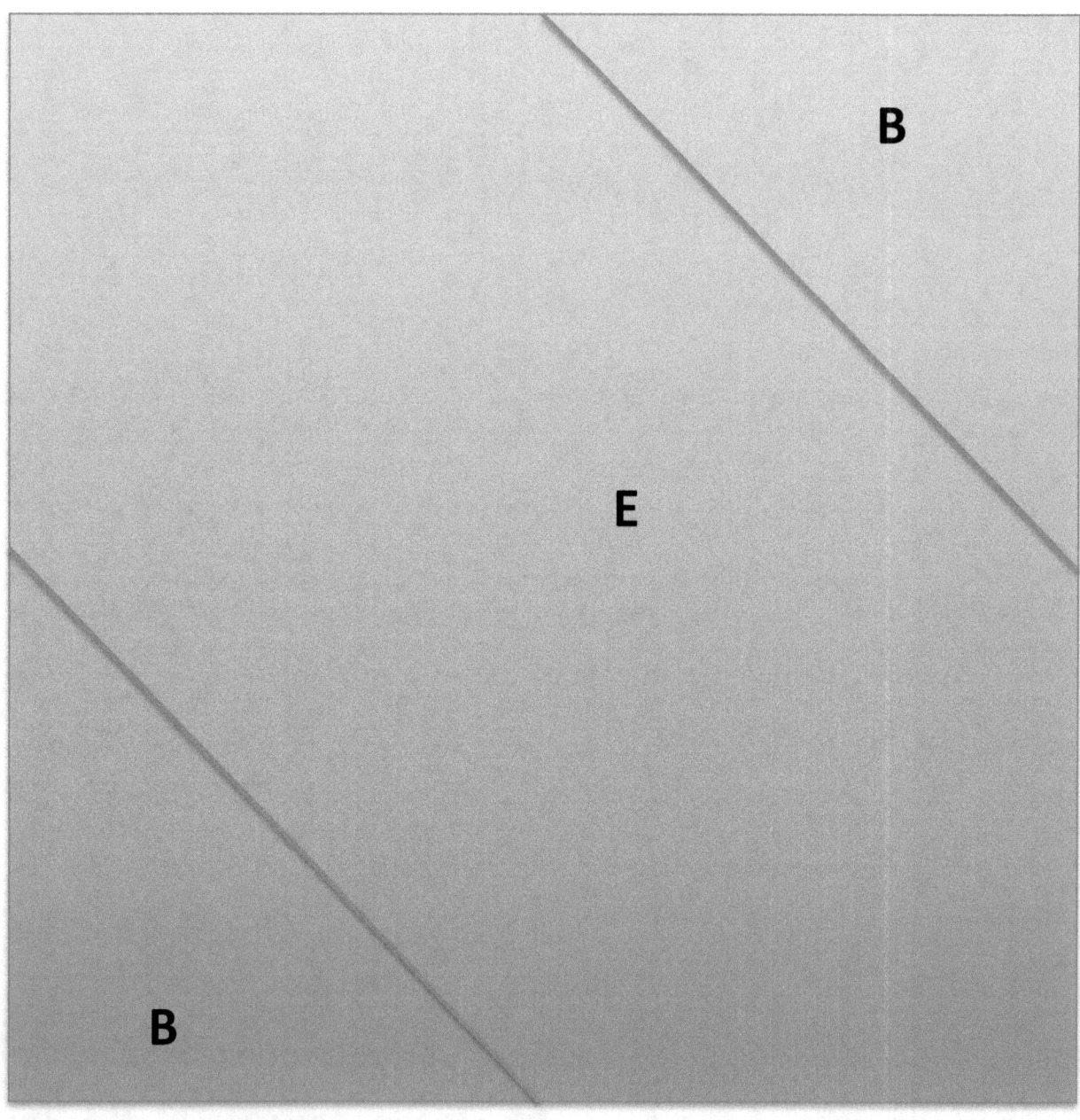

16

COOPERATION SQUARES

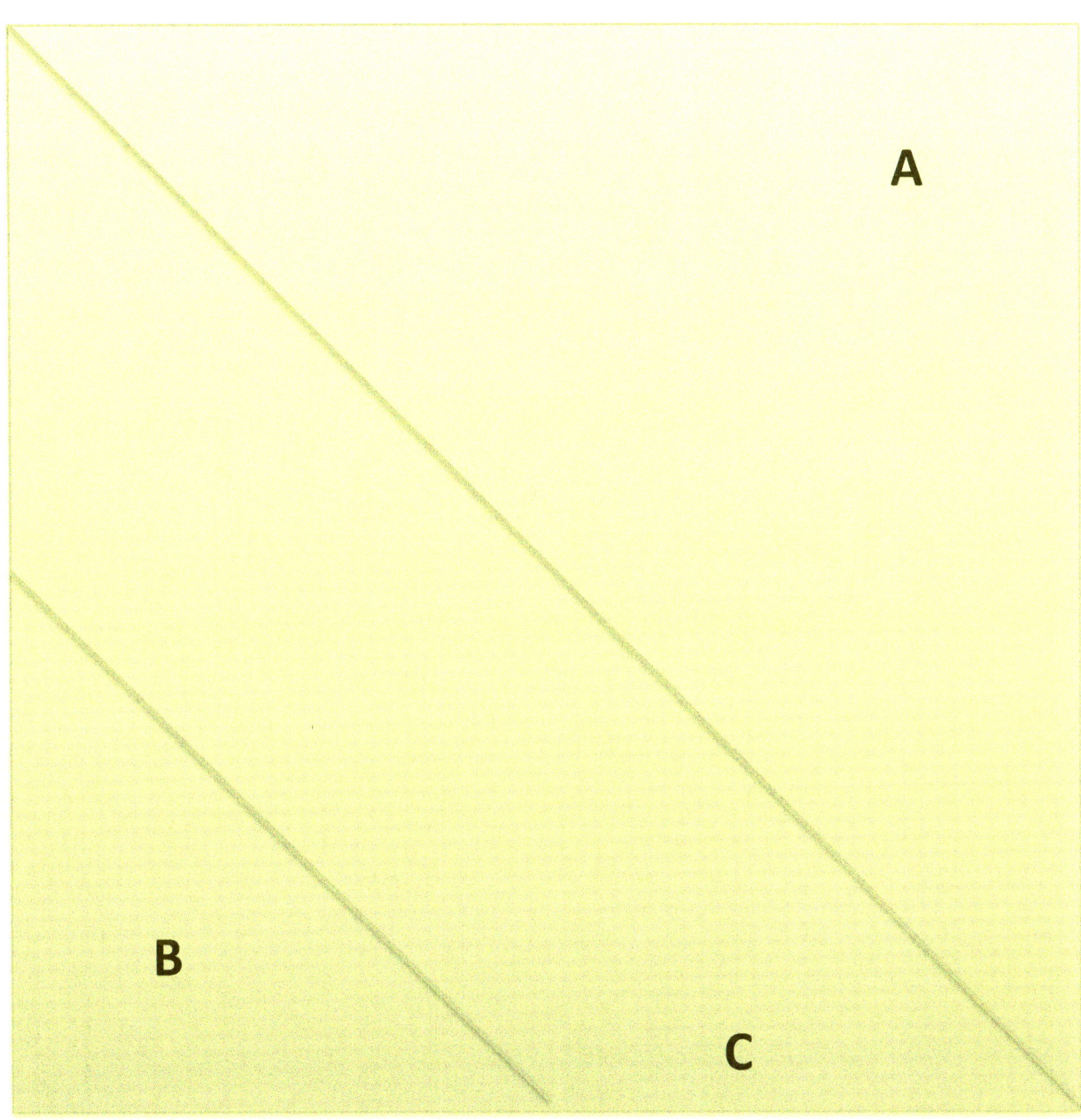

ESSENTIALS #1

COOPERATION SQUARES

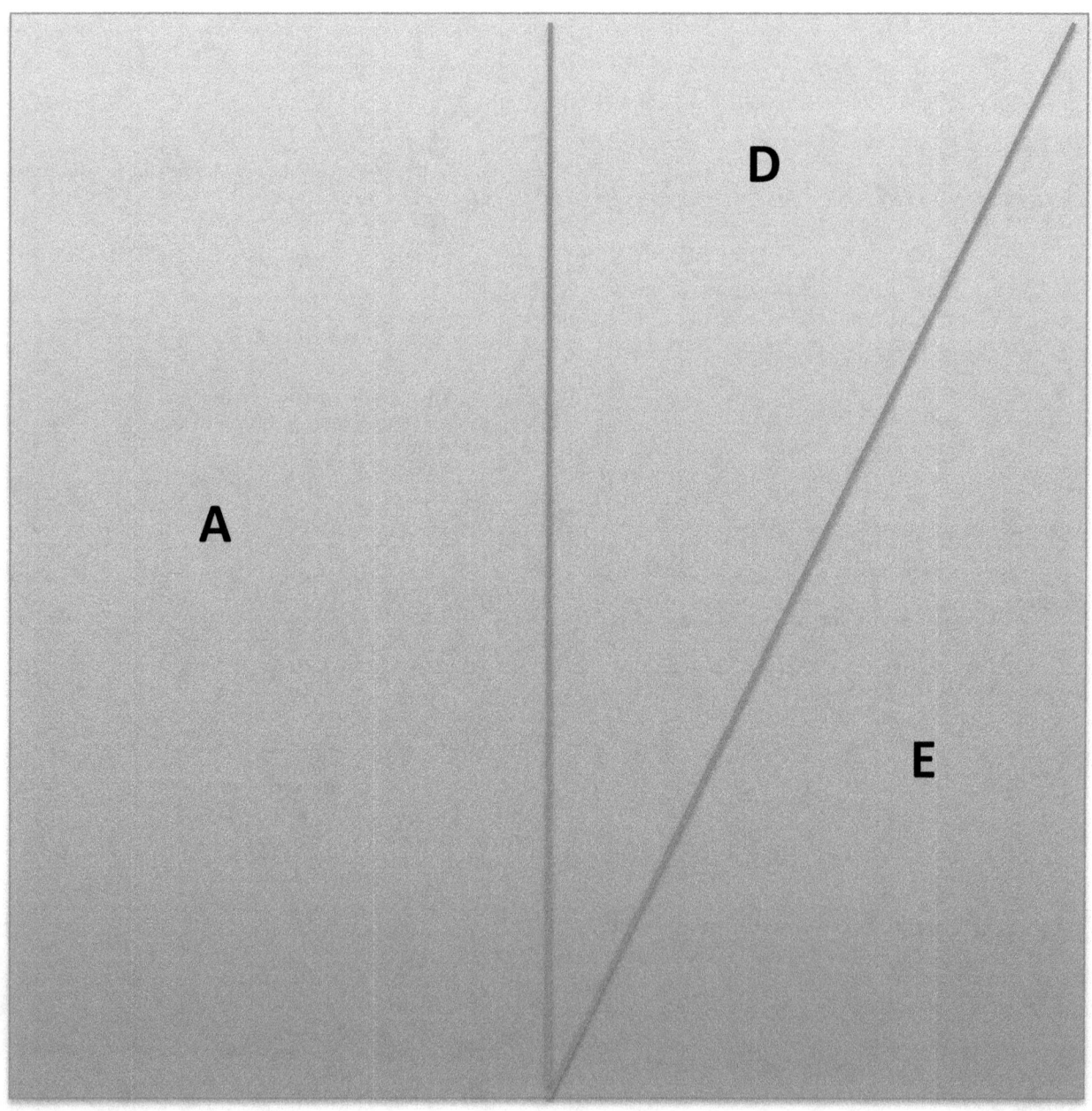

UNDERSTANDING YOUR PERSONALITY

Circle the words that best describe you. If you feel a word does not describe you or only describes you a little, don't circle it. Once you finish, double the number of words you circled in each box and record the number at the bottom of each box. Finally circle your highest box.

Tip: *Do not choose words that describe who you want to be.*
There is no right or wrong answer.

Enjoys instructions	Accurate		Likes authority	Takes charge
Consistent	Controlled		Confident	Determined
Reserved	Predictable		Firm	Controlling
Practical	Orderly		Enjoys challenges	Competitive
Factual	Perfectionist		Problem solver	Productive
Detailed	Analytical		Bold	Purposeful
Precise	Inquisitive		Goal-driven	Adventurous
Scheduled	Sensitive		Strong Willed	Independent
(Beaver) Double your total=			**(Lion) Double your total=**	
Sensitive feelings	Peace Maker		Enthusiastic	Very verbal
Calm	Loyal		Energetic	Takes Risk
Non-demanding	Indecisive		Mixes Easily	Friendly
Enjoys routine	Dislike change		Fun-loving	Enjoys popularity
Warm and relational	Good listener		Spontaneous	Enjoys change
Adaptable	Patient		Creative ideas	Group-oriented
Even Keeled	Thoughtful		Infectious laughter	Sensitive
Give in	Avoids conflict		Motivator	Promoter
(Golden Retriever) Double your total=			**(Otter) Double your total=**	

_____ESSENTIALS #1

PERSONAL STYLES ACTIVITY

1. What are the *strengths* of our style (4 adjectives).

2. What are the *limitations* of our style?

3. What style do we find the most difficult to work with and why?

4. What do other people need to know about us so that we can work together more effectively?

WHICH ANIMAL ARE YOU?

You should have identified a box with your highest score. Some will have two high scores and two low ones. The highest score will represent your highest personality traits.

Below are the descriptions of your animal personality traits. Read the description of your highest score and share your thoughts with others. Your personality is a collection of your emotional and social behavior traits. Your personality describes how others see you and how you present yourself to the world.

 **LION**

This personality likes to take charge. He/she is a powerful leader who loves to be in control. The lion is goal-oriented and swiftly makes decisions with confidence. He/she enjoys new opportunities that lead to advancement and are good problem-solvers especially during difficult situations.

Their Strengths:	Goal-oriented, strong, direct, productive, enjoys challenges, confident
Their environment:	Awards on the wall, Lots of projects, office furniture arranged in a formal way
They Gain Security:	By having control
Their Pace:	Fast and decisive
Their Needs:	Wants others to be efficient and to the point, wants a quick response
They're irritated by:	Slow people, sensitive people, Things that block results

For Growth They Need to:	Be patient with others, appear less demanding, avoid killing morale by being too heavy handed. Avoid taking all the credit for assignments, learn to express grace, be softer and practice shared leadership (let others make decisions). Develop a tolerance for conflict, pace yourself (not too fast).
In Dealing with Them:	Avoid attacking their character, telling them what to do, presenting win-lose scenarios. Give them options and freedom. Be efficient and competent; use facts when you disagree with them, not feelings. Be precise, time-disciplined, and well organized. Don't waste their time. They don't need a lot of information to make a decision

ESSENTIALS #1

BEAVER

Beavers are very organized. He/she doesn't want to do anything the wrong way, they want to do get it right every time. They are perfectionist and take their time to do everything perfectly. They don't like sudden changes and sometimes need reassurance.

Their Strengths:	Hard-working, detailed, accurate, focused on quality not quantity. Have high expectations
Their environment:	Structured and organized, to-do lists, calendars, charts and graphs, functional décor. Formal seating arrangement
They Gain Security:	By being prepared
Their Pace:	Slow and systematic
Their Needs:	Wants a climate that focuses on accuracy and preciseness
They're irritated by:	People that don't know what they are talking about, lack of details, people that don't follow through on their word, surprises,
For Growth They Need to:	Make faster decisions, tolerate conflict, learn to compromise, adjust to change and disorganization. Learn to relax and don't expect others to do things just like they would.
In Dealing with Them:	Avoid criticizing, blunt personal questions, Incomplete or inaccurate recommendations. Give frequent progress reports and reviews. Avoid persuading and don't rush decision-making

GOLDEN RETRIEVER

Golden Retrievers are known as peaceful leaders. They look for appreciation and work best in a less stressful environment with a steady work pattern. He/she is great at making and keeping friends. They are very loyal and do not like big changes. They look for security and can be very sensitive. They love to care for others and be cared for.

Their Strengths: Accommodating, calm, flexible. Possess a great amount of compassion. Listening

Their environment: Family pictures, slogans on the wall, personal items

They Gain Security: Close relationships

Their Pace: Slow and easy

Their Needs: A climate that processes

They're irritated by: Pushy aggressive behavior, insincerity, being the center of attention

For Growth They Need to: Take risks, delegate to others, confront, develop confidence in others, learn to change and adapt. Practice saying no, make firm decisions. Be self-motivated.

In Dealing with Them: Avoid conflict, sudden unplanned risky changes. Give them reassurance, reliability, and assistance in presenting to others. Be non-threatening and sincere. Show interest in their feelings. Don't push. Assure them you will stand behind their decision.

OTTER

Otters are very social creatures. They enjoy being popular and influencing and motivating others. They are the life of the party and are sometimes hurt when others do not like them. They get their energy from being around others and are always ready to have fun with others. They usually have messy rooms and like to hurry to finish jobs.

Their Strengths:	Ability to rally troops to achieve goals or desired outcomes. Positive attitude
Their environment:	Clutter, awards, family pictures, slogans on the wall, friendly
They Gain Security:	Flexibility
Their Pace:	Fast and spontaneous
Their Needs:	A climate that collaborates
They're irritated by:	Too many facts, too much logic, boring tasks, same old approach, routine, being alone, people who are ignoring their opinions
For Growth They Need to:	Respect priorities, more logical approach, follow-through, get better organized, remember commitments, concentrate on the task at hand. Think before they speak and consider consequences before acting or making a decision.
In Dealing with Them:	Avoid negativism, rejection, arguing. Be interested in them. Support their dreams, feelings, and opinions. Do not hurry the discussion. Give them a chance to talk. Don't deal with details. Everyone likes to spend time with Otters, except Beavers.

ESSENTIAL #2

RESPOND SMART

I am in control of my words, actions, attitude, and thoughts (self-control). I think ahead and choose a response that will help me and my surroundings (people, places, and things) become better and not worse. I take responsibility for my actions and you can trust me to do the right thing even when no one is watching (integrity).

Helpful quotes about responding smart:

You must take personal responsibility. You cannot change the circumstances, the seasons, or the wind, but you can change yourself. —Jim Rohn

If you hangout with chickens you're going to cluck, and if you hangout with eagles, you're going to fly. —Steve Maraboli

Respond; don't react, listen; don't talk. Think; don't assume. —Raji Lukkoor

You have control over three things: what you think, what you say, and how you behave. To make a change in your life, you must recognize these gifts are the most powerful tools you possess in shaping the form of your life. —Sonya Friedman

ESSENTIALS #2

RESPOND SMART

Essential question: How valuable is your response as a leader? *Explain with an example.*

Tip: *Greet students with a firm handshake and encourage eye contact to build social intelligence.*

Objective: To demonstrate effective coping skills when faced with a problem

Purpose: Students will be challenged with the task of exercising self-discipline/self control

Vocabulary: Constructive talk   Integrity   Proactive   Reactive

Materials: Proactive vs. Reactive practice sheet with Scenarios
Essential Skill #2-Overview and Quotes

Directions:
1. Read overview and quotes for Essential Skill #2
2. Allow students to have constructive talk with a partner about their favorite quote and explain why. Allow four students to share with the whole group until all quotes have been discussed.
3. Review vocabulary terms as they relate to overview
4. Introduce two methods for responding (Proactive and Reactive)
5. Discuss scenario #1 as a group and complete scenario #2 with a partner.

Conclusion/Evaluation: Discuss responses to scenario #2

Homefun: Reread Sonya Friedman's quote. List 5 things you have control over and 5 things you cannot control. Record this information in your reflection journal including a new insight from today's session.

PROACTIVE VS. REACTIVE

Draw a line to match the antonyms:

Love	Cheap
Peace	Mean
Success	Dishonest
Humble	Insecurity
Security	Failure
Kindness	Impatient
Valuable	Arrogant
Patient	Hate
Honest	Anger

Scenario:

How will you proactively respond to this situation?

- Over time your best friend begins making fun of you and putting you down. She particularly enjoy doing this in front of other students.

- You have asked your brother over and over again not to play with your iPod when you're not home but he does not listen and continues to play with it anyway. You're frustrated. How do you respond?

ESSENTIAL #3

SMART GOALS

I make plans and set goals ahead. I plan to do things that have meaning and connect with my mission. I am important and determined to help make positive changes in my community.

Helpful quotes about smart goals:

Without goals and plans to reach them you are like a ship that has set sail with no destination. —Fitzhugh Dodson

No one can go back and make a brand-new start my friend; but anyone can start from here and make a brand-new end. —Dan Zadra

I alone cannot change the world, but I can cast a stone across the waters to create many ripples. —Mother Teresa

If you aim at nothing you'll hit it every time. —Zig Ziglar

SMART GOALS (PART 1)

Essential Question: How can setting goals lead to a successful postsecondary education, career, and life?

Welcome/Review: Share with a partner the Homefun activity (3 examples of your proactive and reactive responses)

Objective: To understand the importance of setting and achieving short and long term goals with an emphasis on short term goals.

Purpose: To enhance academic achievement by demonstrating the use of critical thinking skills to make informed decisions

Vocabulary: Short term goal   Long term goal   Prioritizing
Emotional goals   Career goals   Physical Goals
Achievable Goals

Materials: Abstract puzzle (1 per group) or any puzzle. Puzzle Key (1 per group)
Setting Goals for Success Brainstorming Sheet
Essential Skill #3 Overview and Quotes
Scissors

Directions:
1. Distribute one puzzle per group. Give students 5 minutes to complete the puzzle without the puzzle key.
2. After 5 minutes, discuss the challenges of completing the puzzle.
3. Distribute the puzzle key to each group allowing 3 minutes to complete the puzzle. Discuss the outcome. Relate to the Puzzle key as the goal/outcome and the puzzle pieces as the steps or details to accomplishing the goal.
4. Read overview and quotes for Essential Skill #3.
5. Allow students to have constructive talk with a partner about their favorite quote and explain why. Allow four students to share with the whole group until all quotes have been discussed.
6. Brainstorm Achievable short-term goals. Using the "Setting Goals for Success" Brainstorming page, allow time for students to complete Step #1.

Conclusion/Evaluation: Whole group sharing of short-term goals

Homefun: Talk to a trusted adult or friend about keeping you accountable with your short-term goal. Record your thoughts about Smart Plan in your Reflection journal.

ESSENTIALS #3

SETTING GOALS FOR SUCCESS

Goal setting is an important skill. This skill will help you accomplish many tasks, big and small. Short term goals helps us to accomplish task in a short period of time and long term goals help us accomplish task over a period of weeks, months, or even years.

Name_____ Date_____

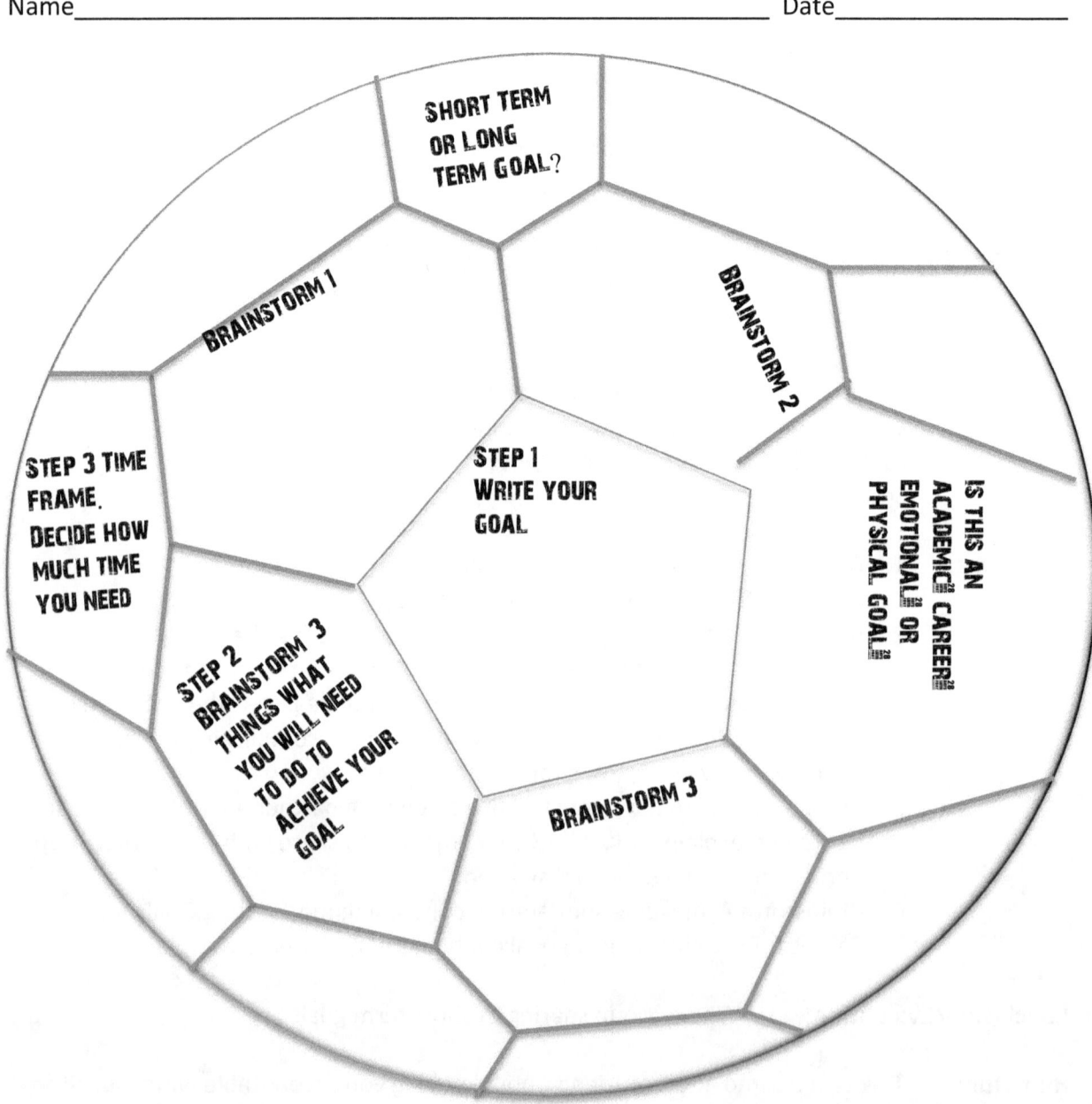

Copyright @ 2016 [Patricia L. Russell, ED.S]. All Rights Reserved.
This material is not to be used or duplicated without consent from Patricia L. Russell.

PUZZLE KEY

Group activity: make copies, cut each shape and allow students 5mins to complete the abstract puzzle without the puzzle key. After 5mins allow any unsuccessful groups to use the answer key to complete the puzzle. Finally, explain the importance of goal setting and having a plan to successfully accomplish goals.

ESSENTIALS #3

SMART GOALS (PART 2)
WITH THE CHA-CHA SLIDE DANCE

Essential Question: How can setting goals lead to a successful postsecondary education, career, and life?

Welcome/Review: Review overview of short-term goals and vocabulary from last week.

Objective: To understand the importance of setting and achieving short and long term goals with an emphasis on short term goals.

Purpose: To enhance academic achievement by demonstrating how using critical thinking skills to make informed decisions will lead to ownership of one's life.

Vocabulary: Short-term goal   Long-term goal   Prioritizing
Emotional goals   Career goals   Physical Goals
Achievable Goals

Materials: "Setting Goals for Success Brainstorming" Sheet
"Cha Cha Slide" on YouTube

Directions:
1. Ask students to participate using movements to the Cha Cha Slide Dance. Afterwards, students will discuss how the song relates to goal-setting.
2. Explain the importance of setting specific steps to support the overall goal.
3. Allow time for students to list 3 action steps to achieve their goal.
4. Allow students to have constructive talk with a partner about their action steps for feedback.

Conclusion/Evaluation: What are some tips that could help you prioritize accomplishing your goal? (Ex., Watching only 30 minutes of TV per day.)

Homefun: Talk to a trusted adult or friend about keeping you accountable for your short-term goal.

Copyright @ 2016 [Patricia L. Russell, ED.S]. All Rights Reserved.
This material is not to be used or duplicated without consent from Patricia L. Russell.

ESSENTIAL #4

PLAN SMART

I recognize the things and people that are most important to me and put them first. I manage my time well by making a schedule and following my plan. I say "no" to the things that distract me from completing my goals. I practice completing the hard work first and the easier things last.

Helpful quotes about planning smart:

If you don't design your own life plan, chances are you'll fall into someone else's plan. And guess what they have planned for you? Not Much. —Jim Rohn

Actions express priorities. —Mahatma Gandhi

Things that matter most must never be at the mercy of things which matter least. —Johann Wolfgang von Goethe

People with goals succeed because they know where they're going. —Earl Nightingale

ESSENTIALS #4

PLAN SMART

Essential Question: How can setting goals lead to a successful postsecondary education, career, and life?

Welcome/Review: What did we learn about goal setting last week?

Objective: To demonstrate an understanding that post-secondary education and life-long learning are necessary for long-term career success.

Purpose: To expand students' vision socially, emotionally, and behaviorally by brainstorming and setting long-term goals for their future.

Vocabulary: <u>Post-secondary Education</u>   <u>Long-term goal</u>   <u>Prioritizing</u>
<u>Career goals</u>   <u>Achievable Goals</u>   <u>Vision</u>

Materials: Goal Organizer.
Story: "What Do You Do With An Idea?" by Kobi Yamada or video of the story can be found on YouTube
Story Talk
Essential Skill #4 Overview and Quotes

Directions:
1. Read or listen to the video of the story "What do you do with an idea"?
2. Allow students to interview a partner about the story "What Do You Do With an Idea?"
3. Read overview and quotes for Essential Skill #4.
4. Allow students to have constructive talk with a partner about their favorite quote and explain why. Allow four students to share with the whole group until all quotes have been discussed.
5. Whole group brainstorm achievable long-term goals and each student records a personal long-term goal.
6. Using the same steps as short-term goals, complete the Goal Organizer.

Conclusion/Evaluation: Why is it important to dream?

Homefun: Complete step #1 through #4 if not completed during the leadership session. Talk to a trusted adult or friend about your long-term goal.

GOAL ORGANIZER

NAME_____ DATE _____

Time to complete goal:

GOAL:

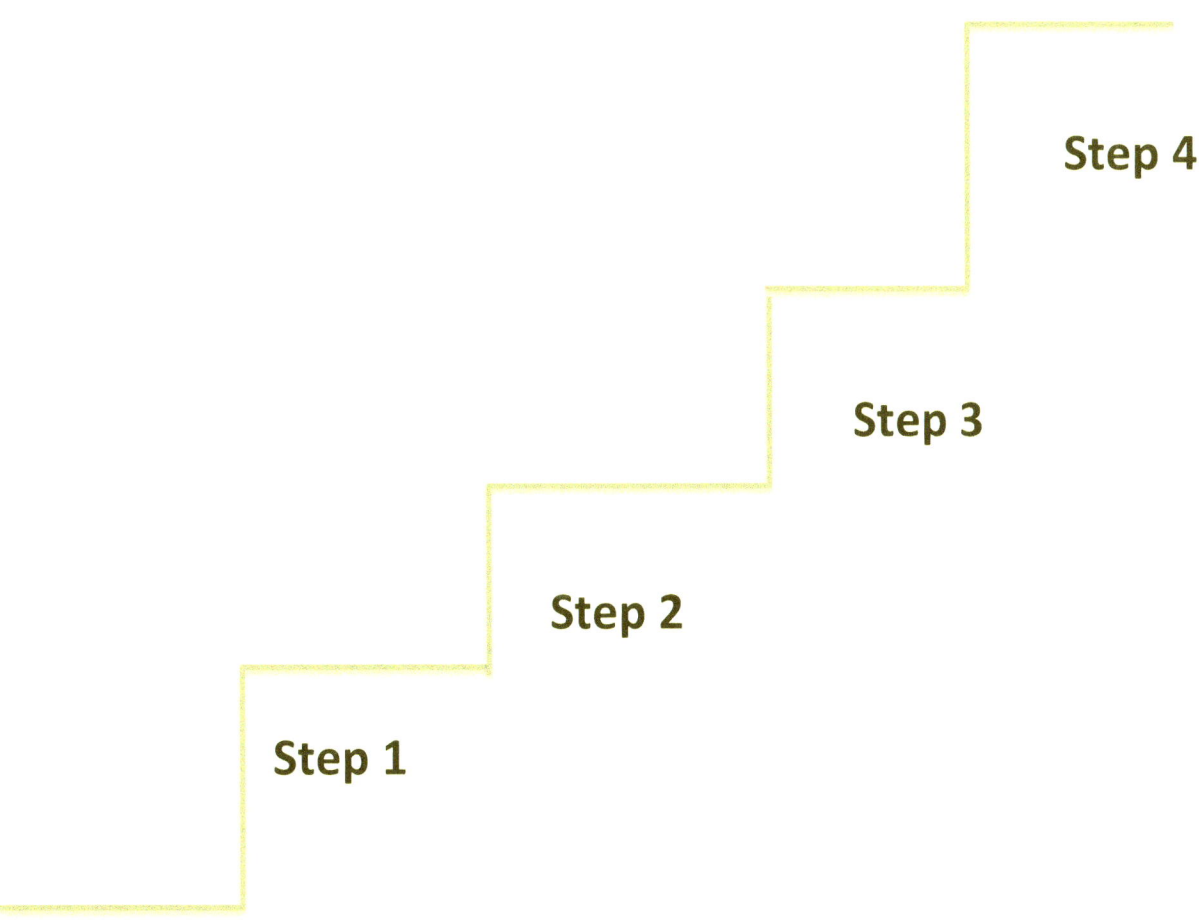

ESSENTIALS #4

STORY TALK

Student Name_____

Name of Story_____

What is the major conflict within this story?
_____
_____
_____
_____

How did the boy feel about his idea at the beginning of the story?
_____
_____
_____
_____

How do the boy's feelings in beginning of the story compare with his feelings at the end of the story? Supports your answer with details from the story.
_____
_____
_____
_____

What happens to the boy's idea?
_____
_____
_____
_____

How does this story relate to goal-setting and the success of your future?
_____
_____
_____
_____

Copyright @ 2016 [Patricia L. Russell, ED.S]. All Rights Reserved.
This material is not to be used or duplicated without consent from Patricia L. Russell.

ESSENTIAL #5

SMART VICTORIES

I understand that people have different wants, expectations, values, and needs and this sometimes causes conflict. I consider fair solutions with integrity to resolve conflicts; solutions that lead to smart victories for all and not failure.

Helpful quotes about smart victories:

Strong people don't put others down... They lift them up.
—Michael P. Watson

The quality of our lives depends not on whether or not we have conflicts, but on how we respond to them. —Tom Crum

Alone we can do so little; together we can do so much.
—Helen Keller

Effective people are not problem-minded; they're opportunity-minded. They feed opportunities and starve problems. They think preventively. —Peter Drucker

ESSENTIALS #5

SMART VICTORIES (PART 1)

Essential Question: Is conflict good or bad? Why?

Welcome/Review: Allow students time to share any of their success stories with short-term goals. Have you accomplished any goals since our last meeting?

Objective: To demonstrate an understanding of effective ways to resolve and prevent conflict using five key strategies.

Purpose: Students will acquire an understanding of ones' self as an individual and a contributing member of a diverse, local, and global community.

Vocabulary: <u>Conflict</u> <u>Compromise</u> <u>Mediator</u>
<u>Cooperate</u>

Materials: Essential Skill #5-Overview
Smart Victories Helpful Solutions for Conflict
Think Smart Victories sheet

Directions:
1. Read overview and quotes for Essential Skill #5
2. Allow students to have constructive talk with a partner about their favorite quote and explain why. Allow four students to share with the whole group until all quotes have been discussed.
3. Introduce five key solutions for supporting smart victories
4. Whole group discusses #1 scenario. Brainstorm ideas for resolving the problem as a win/win, lose/lose, or win/lose
5. Complete scenario #2 in small groups

Conclusion/Evaluation: Think about a conflict that you've had recently. Did you resolve the issue using win/win? Try to practice win/win this week.

Homefun: Complete #3 scenario. Devise your own scenario of a conflict and resolve it with win/win, lose/win, and lose/lose.

SMART VICTORIES (PART 2)

Essential Question: Is Conflict good or bad? Why?

Welcome/Review: Allow students time to share any of their success stories about "Smart Victories".

Objective: To demonstrate an understanding of effective ways to resolve and prevent conflict using five key strategies.

Purpose: Students will acquire an understanding ones self as an individual and a contributing member of a diverse, local, and global community

Vocabulary: Conflict   Compromise   Mediator
Cooperate

Materials: Essential Skill #5- Overview
Smart Victories Helpful Solutions for Conflict
Chart paper per group

Directions:
1. Allow students to work in groups of 5 or 6.
2. Give each group a sheet of chart paper.
3. Review the five key solutions for supporting "Smart Victories".
4. Each group should create a scenario resolving the conflict using 3 of the 5 strategies.
5. Bonus: add an outcome for win/win, win/lose, and lose/lose

Tip: Each group should choose a "Presenter" and a "Scribe". Students should practice speaking to an audience using eye contact and a loud speaking voice.

Conclusion/Evaluation: Allow time for each group to share their scenario, solutions, and outcomes.

Homefun: Record areas of growth/need improvement for Smart Victories in your reflection journal.

SMART VICTORIES

To understand "Smart Victories," let's first make sure we understand conflict and solutions.

<u>Conflict</u> — a disagreement, argument, or fight

HELPFUL SOLUTIONS FOR CONFLICT:

- **<u>Compromise</u>** — Give something so everybody gets something they want.
- **<u>Cooperation</u>** — Work together.
- **<u>Listen up</u>** — Give someone else a chance to speak and pay attention to what they say.
- **<u>Mediator</u>** — Ask someone to help you solve a conflict.
- **<u>Talk it out</u>** — Let someone else know how you feel and what you think.

THINK SMART VICTORIES

1. You and your sister are buying a birthday present for your mom. You have ten dollars and your brother has six. You plan to combine your money and buy one present together. You want to buy perfume. Your sister wants to buy a purse. You don't like you sister's idea, and she doesn't like yours. How would you solve this problem?

   Win/Lose_____
   Lose/Lose_____
   Win/Win_____

2. Amy and I live across the street from one another and we always play together. Today at school we had a test and she wanted to look at my paper for answers. But when I told her no, she took my paper and copied my work. When the teacher caught her she said I let her copy and my consequence was an "F" on my test. How would you solve this problem?

   Win/Lose_____
   Lose/Lose_____
   Win/Win_____

HOME FUN

3. Using your understanding of Smart Victories, devise your own scenario of a conflict. For the scenario, explain a win/lose, lose/lose, and win/win outcome.
   Your scenario:

   Win/Lose_____
   Lose/Lose_____
   Win/Win_____

ESSENTIAL #6

SMART TALK

I realize that listening is sometimes more important than speaking. Understanding others' perspective and their viewpoint helps my mindset grow. I listen first with my whole body (ears, mouth, body, and heart) without interrupting, then speak my words to share my ideas.

Helpful quotes about smart talk:

We have two ears and one mouth so that we can listen twice as much as we speak. —Epictetus

The quieter you become the more you can hear. —Ram Dass

The ear of the leader must ring with the voices of the people. —Woodrow Wilson

The most basic of all human needs is the need to understand and be understood. The best way to understand people is to listen to them. —Ralph Nicols

SMART TALK

Essential Question: How would the world change if people really listened to one another?

Welcome/Review: Students will write on Chart paper or a post-it note any smart victories they had over the week in the designated area (home, school, and community). Then all students should take 3-5 minutes to view the collection of smart victories from the group.

Objective: Students will understand and demonstrate skills of an effective communicator.

Purpose: To participate effectively in a range of conversations with diverse partners, by listening, building on others' ideas, and expressing their own ideas clearly.

Vocabulary: Viewpoint   Perspective   Mindset   Body language

Materials: Essential Skill #6-Overview and Quotes
Speed Chatting: Presentation and Listening Tips
Chart paper per group or post-it notes
"Speed Chat" Activity Instructions

Directions:
1. Read overview and quotes for Essential Skill #6
2. Allow students to have constructive talk with a partner about their favorite quote and explain why. Allow four students to share with the whole group until all quotes have been discussed.
3. Review vocabulary terms as they relate to overview.
4. Introduce "Speed Chatting" (see attachment)

Tip: Remind students that a good listener listens with their eyes, ears, body, and mind.

Conclusion/Evaluation: Have a discussion about what happened. What was challenging? What does it take to be a great listener and a great presenter/speaker? Encourage students to refer back to the presenter and listening tips.

Homefun: Practice smart talk with someone in your community. Record areas of growth/need improvement for Smart Talk in your reflection journal.

ESSENTIALS #6

ACTIVITY: SPEED CHATTING

Objective:
- Student should be able to listen attentively with appropriate eye contact and body language.
- Student should be able to retell what they heard accurately with appropriate details.
- Student should be able to present with a clear speaking voice, appropriate body language, and on topic for the allocated time.

Set up:
1. Choose 2 or 3 questions/prompts. Examples are listed below.
2. Have students choose a partner and number off partner 1 and 2. The pair of students should sit criss cross facing one another.

Directions:
1. Ask the group a question or allow students to make up their own question. Partner 1 will begin as the listener. Partner 2 will have 1 minute to explain their answer. Tell the students, only partner one can talk. Partner 2 must be silent and listen. Set a timer for one minute.
Once the timer goes off, immediately set the timer to 30 seconds and tell partner 2 to repeat/tell back everything partner one told them in as much detail as possible.
2. Switch. Repeat #1 but switch roles so that partner 2 talks and partner 1 listens with the same question.
3. Finally, each student should have a "Listening and Presenting Tips" sheet. Allow each student 30 seconds to share and record feedback with their partner using the listening and speaking tips provided.
4. Before repeating the activity with new questions, have students change partners.

Conclusion/Evaluation:
Have a discussion about what was challenging? What does it take to be a great listener? A great presenter/speaker? Encourage students to refer back to the rubric.

Example questions:
1. Tell your partner about your favorite book. Give as many details as possible.
2. Describe your best friend without saying their name. What makes them a good friend?
3. Describe your favorite vacation? Discuss the location and experienced activities.

SPEED CHATTING/ LISTENING TIPS

Student Name: _____

Circle any area for improvement. Underline any area of strength.

Listens intently to his/her partner. Does not make distracting noises or movements.

Establishes eye contact with his/her partner during the presentation.

Student is able to accurately retell almost ALL information shared by his/her partner.

SPEED CHATTING: PRESENTATION TIPS

Student Name: _____

Circle any area for improvement. Underline any area of strength.

Speaks clearly ALL of the time and is easy to understand.

Eye contact and body language generate a strong interest and enthusiasm about the topic in his/her partner.

Stays on topic the Entire time.

ESSENTIAL #7

SMART LIFE

Living a healthy lifestyle is my goal. I practice healthy habits for my body, mind, heart, and soul by managing my time to do the following: exercise, eat healthy, rest, share time with family and close friends, learn new things, and help others. These things help bring balance to my life and make me a better person.

Helpful quotes about living a smart life:

If I had eight hours to chop down a tree, I'd spend six sharpening my axe. —Abraham Lincoln

When you stop chasing the wrong things, you give the right things a chance to catch you. —Lolly Daskal

Live and work but do not forget to play, to have fun in life and really enjoy it. —Eileen Caddy

Take rest; a field that has rested gives a bountiful crop. —Ovid

SMART LIFE

Essential Question: How can you be the best to others when you don't take care of yourself?

Welcome/Review: Discuss any "smart" celebrations from the previous week.

Objective: Students will identify and classify effective strategies for living a healthy lifestyle by discussing healthy habits for the mind, body, heart, and soul.

Purpose: Students will demonstrate the relationship between education, work, and life experiences and how they impact the global community.

Vocabulary: Soul   Mind   Body   Heart

Materials: Essential Skill #7- Overview and Quotes
Markers
Chart paper per group or post-it notes

Directions:
1. Read overview and quotes for Essential Skill #7
2. Allow students to have constructive talk with a partner about their favorite quote and explain why. Allow four students to share with the whole group until all quotes have been discussed.
3. Review vocabulary terms as they relate to overview.
4. Hang four chart papers on the wall, one for each aspect of a balanced life (mind, body, heart, and soul)
5. Divide students into four groups. Assign each group an aspect for a balanced life then allow each group to brainstorm and write strategies for practicing a healthy lifestyle as it relates to their assigned aspect.
6. Rotate groups to a different chart paper (aspect) every 5 minutes.
7. Once all groups are allowed to rotate and record strategies on each chart, lead a whole group discussion about how to use the strategies.

Tip: Allow 5 or more markers per group. Encourage students to read and discuss strategies before recording.

Conclusion/Evaluation: Whole group: What strategies are you practicing for a smart life? What strategies should you practice more for a smart life? Record your responses to Smart Talk in your reflection journal

Homefun: No Homefun

ESSENTIAL #8

BRAVE VOICE

I think about my words inside my head before I let them out of my mouth. I understand my words are so important that they can create something amazing or cause destruction. I share my ideas with confidence and understand when to hold my words and listen to the words of others.

Helpful quotes about using your brave voice:

Be brave, fight for what you believe in and make your dreams your reality. —Jared Leto

The tongue has no bones, but is strong enough to break a heart. So be careful with your words. —Proverbs

Have the courage to follow your heart and intuition. They somehow already know what you truly want to become. —Steve Jobs

Raise your words not your voice, it is rain that grows flowers not thunder. —Rumi

BRAVE VOICE

Essential Question: How can you be the best to others when you don't take care of yourself?

Welcome/Review: Recall any "smart" celebrations from the previous week. Review expectations from the Brave Voice Rubric

Objective: Students will demonstrate effective public speaking skills according to the "Brave Voice Rubric."

Purpose: Students will demonstrate the relationship between education, work, and life experiences and how they impact the global community.

Vocabulary: Confidence   destruction

Materials: Essential Skill #8-Overview and Quotes
Brave Voice Rubric
Final "Leadership Journey Story"

Directions:
1. Read overview and quotes for Essential Skill #8
2. Allow students to have constructive talk with a partner about their favorite quote and explain why. Allow four students to share whole group until all quotes have been discussed.
3. Review vocabulary terms as they relate to overview
4. Divide students into groups with no more than 6 students per group. Each student should have 6 copies of the Brave Voice Rubric.
5. Each student will present their final Leadership Journey Story while others in the group listen then score their presentation according to the rubric.
6. After each presentation students will share "two stars and a wish" for each student (stars=compliments, wish= a tip for improvement) then submit all scored rubrics to the presenting student for their review.

Tip: This process could take two to three weeks to complete all presentations.

Conclusion/Evaluation: Please allow each presenting student 5 minutes to present and listening students 3 to 5 minutes to score

Homefun: Presenting students should write a response in their reflection journal. How will I use the information I learned through this leadership program to help me have a successful future?

BRAVE VOICE RUBRIC

Student Name_____

Scored by_____

Circle the student's performance for each category.

CATEGORY	4	3	2	1
Ideas were clearly presented and exciting	Speaks clearly and distinctly ALL of the time with expression in voice.	Speaks clearly and distinctly with some expression in voice.	Speaks clearly but voice is not distinct MOST of the time and no expression.	Often mumbles or can not be understood.
Connected with the audience with good body language (eye contact and confident posture)	Eye contact and body language generate a strong interest and enthusiasm about the topic in his/her partner. Good posture	Eye contact and body language generate some interest and enthusiasm about the topic in his/her partner.	Eye contact and body language are used to try to generate enthusiasm, but do not seem genuine. Slouched posture	Very little or no use of eye contact or body language. Did not generate much interest in topic being presented. Slouched posture
Listened to feedback with a good and open attitude	Welcomed feedback with comments and a positive attitude	Welcomed some feedback. Seemed somewhat uncomfortable with some feedback.	Not welcoming or comfortable with feedback.	Angry or negative about feedback.

BONUS LESSON

ENTREPRENEURSHIP

I am not afraid to dream big or think extraordinary thoughts. I will risk opportunities to be successful even if I fail. I understand that failure makes me stronger. I am willing to work hard and effectively with a team to create a plan that will help me live out my passion. I refuse to be defeated by fear or my weaknesses.

Helpful quotes about entrepreneurship:

I create. I take risk. I live my passion. I am an entrepreneur.
—Unknown

Do not be embarrassed by your failures, learn from them and start again. —Richard Branson, founder of the Virgin Group

Always deliver more than expected. —Larry Page, Co-founder of Google

When you are ready to quit you're closer than you think.
—Bob Parsons, Founder of GoDaddy

BONUS SKILL: A GROWTH MINDS.E.T.
STUDENT ENTREPRENEURS of TOMORROW

Essential Question: How would you use your ideas and dreams to solve problems in the world?

Welcome/Review: Discuss any "smart" celebrations from the previous week.

Objective: Students will brainstorm solutions to challenges we face at our school everyday and develop possible ideas to solve these challenges

Purpose: Students will acquire and utilize the knowledge, attitudes, critical thinking, self-directed, and collaborative learning techniques necessary for academic achievement.
W.3.2 Write informative/explanatory texts to examine a topic and convey ideas and information clearly.
SL.3.1 Engage effectively in a range of collaborative discussions with diverse partners on grade level topics and text building on others' ideas and expressing their own clearly.
SL.3.6 Speak in complete sentences when appropriate to task and situation in order to provide requested details or clarification

Vocabulary: Entrepreneur   Empathy   Innovation   Inspiration

Materials: A Different MindS.E.T. overview and quotes
Challenge Sheet
Inspiration/Empathy sheet
Requested material from student list
Growth MindS.E.T. Rubric

Directions: Watch the video, "Kid President Has A Dream" (optional)
1. Read overview and quotes for A Different Mind S.E.T.
2. Allow students to have constructive talk with a partner about their favorite quote and explain why. Allow four students to share with the whole group until all quotes have been discussed.
3. Review vocabulary terms as they relate to overview.
4. Review and hand-out Growth Mind S.E.T. Rubric with class
5. Divide students into groups of five. Give each group a Challenge and Inspiration/Empathy Sheet.

6. Ask students to discuss problems, dreams, and concerns about their school. Ask students to choose and record one problem pre group as their focus for design on the Challenge sheet. (10mins)
7. Students should individually discuss and record observations, feelings, and reflections about the challenge.

Tip: Allow 5-10 minutes each for students to complete Challenge and Inspiration/Empathy sheet. Encourage students to discuss ideas before recording.

Conclusion/Evaluation: Students will clearly share their understanding of why the design/idea is needed.

Homefun: Complete Inspiration/Empathy sheet if not completed during the leadership session.

BONUS LESSON: ENTREPRENEURSHIP

A GROWTH MINDS.E.T. (PART 2)
STUDENT ENTREPRENEURSHIP TOMORROW

Essential Question: How would you use your ideas and dreams to solve problems in the world?

Welcome/Review: Whole group: Allow each group to share their focus challenge and Inspiration/Empathy for design

Objective: Students will brainstorm solutions to challenges we face at our school everyday and develop possible ideas to solve these challenges

Purpose: Students will acquire and utilize the knowledge, attitudes, critical thinking, self-directed, and collaborative learning techniques necessary for academic achievement.
W.3.2 Write informative/explanatory texts to examine a topic and convey ideas and information clearly.
SL.3.1 Engage effectively in a range of collaborative discussions with diverse partners on grade level topics and text building on others' ideas and expressing their own clearly.
SL.3.6 Speak in complete sentences when appropriate to task and situation in order to provide requested details or clarification.

Vocabulary: <u>Entrepreneur</u>   <u>Empathy</u>   <u>Innovation</u>   <u>Inspiration</u>

Materials: A Different MindS.E.T. overview and quotes
Reflection sheet
Innovation sheet
Design/Experiment sheet
Request material from student list

Directions:
1. Ask students to discuss insights and new findings from each student's Inspiration page within their small group. Students should record common observations and reflections on their Reflection Sheet.
2. Ask students to brainstorm big ideas about solutions and needs to their problem, then choose and record one idea and need on their Innovation Sheet to design and experiment.
3. Using materials provided, students will construct and/or illustrate their design, then complete the Design/Experiment Sheet.

Tip: Allow 5-10 minutes each for students to complete Innovation and Experiment Sheet. Encourage students to discuss ideas before recording.

Conclusion/Evaluation: Students will practice clearly explaining their understanding of why the design was a success or not.

Homefun: Complete Innovation and/or Experiment Sheet if not completed during the leadership session.

BONUS LESSON: ENTREPRENEURSHIP

A GROWTH MINDS.E.T. (PART 3)
STUDENT ENTREPRENEURSHIP TOMORROW

Essential Question: How would you use your ideas and dreams to solve problems in the world?

Welcome/Review: Whole group: Allow each group to share their focus challenge and Inspiration/Empathy for design

Objective: Students will brainstorm solutions to challenges we face at our school everyday and develop possible ideas to solve these challenges.

Purpose: Students will acquire and utilize the knowledge, attitudes, critical thinking, self-directed, and collaborative learning techniques necessary for academic achievement.
W.3.2 Write informative/explanatory texts to examine a topic and convey ideas and information clearly.
SL.3.1 Engage effectively in a range of collaborative discussions with diverse partners on grade level topics and text building on others ideas and expressing their own clearly.
SL.3.6 Speak in complete sentences when appropriate to task and situation in order to provide requested details or clarification.

Vocabulary:

Materials: A Different MindS.E.T. Rubric (one per group)

Directions:
1. Ask each group to present their design explaining their understanding of why it is important and the success of their idea.

Conclusion/Evaluation: Record your experience from this lesson in your Reflection Journal.

BONUS LESSON: ENTREPRENEURSHIP

CHALLENGE

Think of a problem at our school that you have noticed and would like to find a solution.
_____
_____
_____
_____
_____

List your dreams and concerns for this problem:

Dreams	Concerns
1.	
2.	
3.	
4.	
5.	

Complete the sentence using your challenge/design idea

How might we_____
_____
_____
_____
_____

BONUS LESSON: ENTREPRENEURSHIP

INSPIRATION/EMPATHY

Connect with the people that will benefit from your design or idea. Interview at least two people within your group.

What problems have you observe at school?
_____
_____
_____

How would you like to see the problem resolved?
_____
_____
_____

Who is mostly affected by this problem?
_____
_____
_____

How have you been affected by this problem?
_____
_____
_____

How would our school improve if this problem were resolved?
_____
_____
_____

How would students improve if this problem were resolved?
_____
_____
_____

REFLECTIONS

Reflect on the information you collected from Inspiration/Empathy.

What common ideas did you find?

_____
_____
_____
_____
_____
_____

What do you think is most important according to your insight from Inspiration/Empathy?

_____
_____
_____
_____
_____
_____

What can you conclude?

_____
_____
_____
_____
_____
_____

BONUS LESSON: ENTREPRENEURSHIP

INNOVATION
BRAINSTORM AND BIG IDEAS

Insert four big ideas for your challenge
Based on the information recorded in Reflections

Insert four needs for your challenge
Based on the information recorded in Reflections.

Complete the sentence using only one need and big idea.

How might we _____?
                            (need)

How might we _____?
                           (big idea)

DESIGN/EXPERIMENT

Create a draft of a design then construct a design for an experiment.

Sketch 2 rough drafts of your design. Share your drafts with your group for feedback and ideas for improvement.

Re-create your final draft adding any corrections.

Build your design using materials provided. Be creative, not perfect, with materials.

DEVELOPING A WINNER'S ATTITUDE

DEVELOPING A WINNER'S ATTITUDE #1

IMPULSE CONTROL

I stop and think about what could happen then ask myself if that is the outcome I want. I practice the ability to restrain my feelings, impulses, thoughts, and words for my best interest and the best interest of others.

Helpful quotes about impulse control:

Self control is knowing you can... but deciding you won't
—A. Poster

Control your own destiny or someone else will. —Jack Welch

I will not stress myself out about things I can't control or change. —Unknown

A man without self-control is like a city without walls.
—Proverbs 25:28

DEVELOPING A WINNER'S ATTITUDE #1

IMPULSE CONTROL

Essential Question: If choices equal power, describe the power you have in your life.

Welcome/Review: Recall any "smart "celebrations from the previous week. Allow student to complete the "Rating My Impulse Control" self –assessment.

Objective: Students will demonstrate multiple ways to practice self-control.

Purpose: Students will demonstrate appropriate personal safety, responsibility and coping skills that lead to physically and emotionally healthy behaviors.

Vocabulary: Self Discipline Impulse Control

Materials: Impulse Control overview and quotes
The Stop and Think Game
Instructions for Simon Says
Naming the Colors
Rating My Impulse Control self assessment

Directions:
1. Read overview and quotes for Impulse Control
2. Allow students to have constructive talk with a partner about their favorite quote and explain why. Allow four students to share with the whole group until all quotes have been discussed.
3. Review vocabulary terms as they relate to overview
4. Choose two games to play with the whole group. These games will allow students to demonstrate self-control/impulse control.
5. Instructions and games are attached below.

Tip: An important strategy for practicing self-control is to "Stop, Think, Then Act."

Conclusion/Evaluation: Revisit "Rating My Impulse Control Behaviors" self-assessment. Allow students to discuss one impulse behavior for improvement and list strategies to practice for improving this behavior. All answers should be recorded in the Reflection Journal

Homefun: List 5 examples of things you have control over in this world and 5 things you cannot control. Record this information in your Reflection Journal.

IMPULSE CONTROL GAMES

The Stop and Think Game
Students are instructed to do and say certain things. If the instruction is consistent with appropriate school behavior, they are to do it. If they are instructed to do or say something inappropriate, they are to say, "Stop and Think."

Naming the Color
A poster is made with the names of colors; each of the color names is written in a different color. For example, the word "red" is written with a green marker, "yellow" is written with a red marker, "black" is written in blue. Include some color names written in that color ("red" written with a red marker). Students are instructed to name the colors, **Not Read The Words,** in the order they appear on the poster- as fast as they can. This activity helps teach young people the difference between reacting out of habit and stopping to think before reacting.

Simon Says
One person is designated Simon, the others are the players. Standing in front of the group, Simon gives players commands. However, the players must only obey commands that begin with the words "Simon Says." For example, if Simon says, "Simon says touch your toes," then players must touch their toes.

The Stop and Think Game

Students are instructed to do and say certain things. If the instruction is consistent with appropriate school behavior, they are to do it. If they are instructed to do or say something that is inappropriate, they are to say, "Stop and Think."

1. Look to your right
2. Look to your left
3. Give someone a high five
4. Stand up
5. Turn around
6. Scream your name
7. Slap your neighbor
8. Run to the door
9. Sit down
10. Lean back in your chair
11. Hug someone
12. Hit someone
13. Stand up
14. Stand on a chair
15. Shake hands with your neighbor
16. Stick your tongue out
17. Sit down
18. Lay down
19. Close your eyes
20. Take a nap
21. Open your eyes
22. Smile

DEVELOPING A WINNER'S ATTITUDE #1

Naming The Colors

A poster is made with the names of colors; each of the color names is written in a different color. For example, the word "red" is written with a green marker, "yellow" is written with a red marker, "black" is written in blue. Include some color names written in that color ("red" written with a red marker). Students are instructed to name the colors, **Not Read The Words,** in the order they appear on the poster — as fast as they can. This activity helps teach young people the difference between reacting out of habit and stopping to think before reacting.

Pink	**Orange**	**Black**	**Brown**	**Red**
Blue	**Grey**	**Yellow**	**Green**	**Purple**
White	**Brown**	**Red**	**Black**	**Blue**
Orange	**Pink**	**Yellow**	**Green**	**Red**
Purple	**Brown**	**Grey**	**White**	**Green**
Orange	**Yellow**	**Black**	**Brown**	**Blue**

DEVELOPING A WINNER'S ATTITUDE #1

IMPULSE CONTROL BEHAVIORS RUBRIC

Student Name_____

Behavior	5 Excellent	4 Good	3 Fair	2 Not Good	1 Poor
I raise my hand in class before speaking					
I stop myself from interrupting others when they are speaking					
I think of solutions to a problem before I react					
I wait for permission to join in a group or conversation before jumping in					
I ask to play before joining other's game					
I stand patiently in line for my turn at the water fountain					
I think before I respond					
I think before I make a big decision					
I control my anger					
I keep my hands to my self					
I listen to others					
I can sit at my seat or in my space without distracting others while learning					

DEVELOPING A WINNER'S ATTITUDE #2

EMOTIONAL & SOCIAL INTELLIGENCE

I am aware of the feelings of others and myself. I understand how to read nonverbal language and respond appropriately within a large and small group.

Helpful examples of emotional and social intelligence:

- Knowing how to greet others: Properly introducing yourself beginning with a hello, your name, and giving eye contact.

- Demonstrating respect for feelings of others: If someone is crying ask "What's wrong?" or seek help.

- Knowing when and how much to speak in a conversation: Wait for a pause to speak and use a clear speaking voice. Also, give others an opportunity to comment without interrupting.

- Making appropriate comments: Show empathy for a person's feelings and compassion by saying kind things.

- Finding win/win solutions during conflicts with others: If there's a problem, try to compromise so that everyone wins.

EMOTIONAL & SOCIAL INTELLIGENCE

Essential Question: How do you know what to do to fit into different social situations? Do you understand emotional and nonverbal clues?

Welcome/Review: Recall any "smart" celebrations from the previous week.

Objective: Students will make a hypothesis and determine appropriate responses to social behaviors and nonverbal clues by practicing empathy and self-discipline.

Purpose: Students will acquire interpersonal skills that demonstrate respect for all.

Vocabulary: Social Intelligence   Empathy   Nonverbal   Hypothesis

Materials: "Social Intelligence" overview and quotes
"Compassion" activity sheet
Pictures of students with different expressions

Directions:
1. Read overview and quotes for social intelligence
2. Allow students to have constructive talk with a partner about their favorite quote and explain why. Allow four students to share with the whole group until all quotes have been discussed.
3. Whole group discuss feeling words and appropriate reactions. For example, how does a person look when they are feeling angry? How would you respond?
4. Complete the "Compassion" activity sheet together.
5. Next, divide the students into groups of no more than 5 or 6 students and hand each group a picture of a student.
6. Write a scenario about the picture. Identify how the student in the picture feels and what nonverbal clues led you to this conclusion. Lastly, describe how you would respond to this student using Social and Emotional Intelligence.

Tip: If time does not allow for a final whole group discussion, use the information as a review for the following week.

Conclusion/Evaluation: Discuss as a whole group discuss how social intelligences can be used at school and home. Create a list of strategies inside your Reflection Journal.

DEVELOPING A WINNER'S ATTITUDE #2

COMPASSION ACTIVITY

How does the baby feel?
_____
_____
_____
_____

How would you respond?
_____
_____
_____
_____

How does he feel?
_____
_____
_____
_____

How would you respond?
_____
_____
_____
_____

How do they feel?
_____
_____
_____
_____

How would you respond?
_____
_____
_____
_____

DEVELOPING A WINNER'S ATTITUDE #3

GRATITUDE

I recognize what others do for me and I respond with positive actions or words. My friends, family, and community members know that I am a grateful person because I always take the time to express my thanks without expecting anything in return.

Helpful quotes about gratitude:

Feeling gratitude and not expressing it is like wrapping a present and not giving it. —William Arthur Ward

Enjoy the little things, for one day you may look back and realize they were the big things. —Robert Brault

As we express our gratitude, we must never forget that the highest appreciation is not to utter words but to live by them. —John F. Kennedy

He is a wise man who does not grieve for the things which he has not, but rejoices for those which he has. —Epictetus

GRATITUDE

Essential Question: How can gratitude help us become a better person? How can it help us connect to others?

Welcome/Review: Recall any "smart" celebrations from the previous week.

Objective: Students will give examples of multiple ways they can contribute and show appreciation as leaders in their community.

Purpose: Students will demonstrate the relationship between education, work and life experiences and how that impacts the global community.

Vocabulary: Gratitude

Materials: Gratitude overview and quotes
Post-it Notes
Chart paper

Directions:
1. Read overview and quotes for Gratitude
2. Allow students to have constructive talk with a partner about their favorite quote and explain why. Allow four students to share with the whole group until all quotes have been discussed.
3. Divide the chart paper into 4 categories (School/Community/Home/ Friends & Family.
   Discuss a few examples of gratitude as a whole group.
4. Give each student 4 post it notes. Ask students, "What are examples of things you can do at home, school, in your community, and with family and friends to show your gratitude?"
5. After instructions are given, the remaining time is private think and writing time.
6. Once students are finished, allow them to post their post it under the appropriate category.

Tip: If time does not allow for a final whole group discussion, use the information as a review for the following week.

Conclusion/Evaluation: Discuss as a whole group the strategies to practice for improving skills of showing gratitude. Create a list of strategies inside your Reflection Journal.

DEVELOPING A WINNER'S ATTITUDE #4

GRIT

I am determined to achieve my goals. I understand things will not always be easy and sometimes I may lose or need to delay gratification but I will never choose to quit. I will persevere! I will achieve my goals through hard work, focus, and self-motivation. I am determined to succeed!

Helpful quotes about grit:

Talent does not determine success, grit does. —Dillon Williams

I'm not telling you it's going to be easy — I'm telling you it's going to be worth it. —Art Williams

A determined mind and strong will bear endless possibilities. —Unknown

If you can't fly, then run, if you can't run, then walk, if you can't walk, then crawl, but whatever you do, you have to keep moving forward. —Dr. Martin Luther King, Jr.

DEVELOPING A WINNER'S ATTITUDE #4

GRIT: NOW OR LATER?

Essential Question: What do you want so badly that it is so hard for you to wait?

Welcome/Review: Recall any "smart" celebrations from the previous week. Allow students to complete the "Rating My Impulse Control" self assessment.

Objective: Students will develop an understanding of what delaying gratification means.

Purpose: Students will demonstrate appropriate personal safety, responsibility and coping skills that lead to physically and emotionally healthy behaviors.

Vocabulary: Delay   Gratification   Perseverance

Materials: "Grit" overview and quotes; 2 or 3 bags of "Now or Laters" candy or any candy

Directions:
1. Ask students to complete multiplication facts for 2 minutes or jumping jacks. When they finish, tell the students they may have one treat because they finished the task or they can have 3 treats if they will work for 2 more minutes.
2. After the students make their choice, complete any extra math facts or jumping jacks then reward with treats.
3. Allow students to discuss why some students wanted their treat right away and others were willing to wait.
Explain as a whole group, how delaying gratification can help you receive better rewards later.
4. Read overview and quotes for Grit
5. Allow students to have constructive talk with a partner about their favorite quote and explain why. Allow four students to share with the whole group until all quotes have been discussed.
6. Review vocabulary terms as they relate to overview.
7. Allow students to work in pairs to discuss 3 strategies they could use that could help them delay gratification. (Ex. Positive Self talk. It will be better later. Practicing patience is a good leadership skill.)

Conclusion/Evaluation: Whole group, allow students to make a list of strategies for delaying gratification in their Reflection Journal, then circle one or two to practice during the upcoming week.

Homefun: Share your strategies for delaying gratification with others and practice.

Copyright @ 2016 [Patricia L. Russell, ED.S]. All Rights Reserved.
This material is not to be used or duplicated without consent from Patricia L. Russell.

GLOSSARY

Achievable Goals — realistic goals that can be measured by time and ability. To determine if your goals are measurable, ask yourself: How much? How many? How will I know when they are accomplished?

Body — the entire structure of a human being consisting of the head, neck, trunk, arms and hands, legs and feet

Body Language — communicating your thoughts or feelings by the way you place and move your body or show facial expressions

Career goals — planning and setting steps for what you would like to accomplish in your career

Compromise — give something so everybody gets something they want

Confidence — feeling or having self-assurance. Being sure of ones self

Conflict — disagreement, argument, or fight

Constructive Talk — structured conversation with multiple students who are seeking understanding of a specific topic or question.

Cooperate — working together without conflict, harmonious

Delay — to put off until later

Destruction — to tear down or destroy

Empathy — the ability to understand and share the feelings of another

Entrepreneur — a person who organizes and operates their own business

Gratification — pleasure or good feelings gained from the satisfaction of a desire

Gratitude — showing appreciation using words or actions

Heart — a muscular organ about the size of a fist in your chest; strong feelings and kind deeds for others

Hypothesis — an idea or theory that is not proven but that leads to further study or discussion

Innovation — a new idea different from the normal; creative

Inspiration — a mental or divine influence

Impulse Control — the ability or failure to resist temptation

Integrity — the quality of being honest and having strong moral principles

Long-term goal — accomplishing a goal over a period of weeks, months, or even years.

Mediator — someone to help you solve a conflict

Mind — the part of the person that thinks, reasons, feels, and remembers

Mindset — a mental attitude or particular way of thinking

Nonverbal — Communicating your thoughts or feelings by the way you place and move your body or show facial expressions

Perseverance — determination in doing something despite difficulty

Perspective — viewpoint or attitude towards something

Physical Goals — accomplishing a task to improve your physical condition

Post-Secondary Education — any education beyond high school

Prioritizing — the ability to identify and organize important things first

Proactive — Planning ahead

Reactive — Responding to a situation

Self-Discipline — the ability to control one's self

GLOSSARY

Short-term goal — accomplishing a task in a short amount of time

Social Intelligence — the ability to get along well with others, and to get them to cooperate with you

Soul — the spiritual part of a person that is believed to give life to the body

Teamwork — the ability to work together towards a common goal

Viewpoint — a way of looking at or thinking about something

Vision — the act or power of being able to see in the present or future

REFERENCES

Bright Spark/Design Thinking. (2017, June). Retrieved from http://bright spark.org

Copeland, L. (1998). Hunter and His Amazing Remote Control. Chapin, SC: Youthlight.

Smalley, G. (1996). Animal Personality Test [Measurement instrument]. Nashville, TN; Nelson Thomas Inc.

Triganza, A.S. (2009, July 16). Cooperation Squares. Retrieved from http://cpd.yolasitc.com/resources/coopsqurs.pdf

Zentic, T. (2014). Now or Later. Grit & Bear It! (pp. 52-53). Boys Town, NE: Boys Town Press.

ASSESSMENTS

ASSESSMENT

LEADERSHIP EXPERIENCE ASSESSMENT

Student Name_____

1. Compare and contrast qualities of a good team player vs. qualities of a poor team player.

2. Essential #2 reminds us that a leader's response to his/her surroundings is very important. Name three areas of control that a leader should remember before responding to a situation?

3. You want to make an "A" on your multiplication test. List in order of priority four steps you will take to accomplish your goal.

4. Using your understanding of smart victories, devise your own scenario of a conflict. For the scenario explain a win/lose, lose/lose, and win/win outcome.

   Lose/lose

   Win/win

   Lose/win

5. Essential #6 teaches us that listening is sometimes more important than talking. Is this true? Explain.

6. Reflect on your leadership experience and skills you have learned this year. On a separate sheet of paper, explain what you have learned and how you will use this information for your future.

ASSESSMENT

LEADERSHIP EXPERIENCE PARENT SURVEY

1. My student leader showed an increase in the area of responsibility this year.
   Mark only one oval

   Strongly disagree
   Disagree
   Undecided
   Agree
   Strongly agree

2. I feel that the Student Leadership Experience has helped prepare my student with better communication skills for college.
   Mark only one oval

   Strongly disagree
   Disagree
   Undecided
   Agree
   Strongly agree

3. How can we better communicate with parents about weekly updates and student progress?

4. My student leader has a stronger awareness of careers and how to work effectively with others to be successful in life.
   Mark only one oval

   Strongly disagree
   Disagree
   Undecided
   Agree
   Strongly agree

5. How can we improve the Student Leadership Experience?

ASSESSMENT

LEADERSHIP EXPERIENCE TEACHER SURVEY

1. My student leader showed an increase in their ability to think critically this year.

    Mark only one oval

    Strongly disagree
    Disagree
    Undecided
    Agree
    Strongly agree

2. I feel that my student leader has increased in their ability to communicate with others.

    Mark only one oval

    Strongly disagree
    Disagree
    Undecided
    Agree
    Strongly agree

3. How can we better communicate with teachers about weekly updates and student progress?

    My student leader has a stronger awareness of problem solving and collaborating with other.
    Mark only one oval

    Strongly disagree
    Disagree
    Undecided
    Agree
    Strongly agree

4. How can we improve the Student Leadership Academy of Chattanooga?

www.ingramcontent.com/pod-product-compliance
Lightning Source LLC
Chambersburg PA
CBHW060317240426
43661CB00059B/2792